tree top
decorations

tree top decorations

25 dazzling ideas for angels, stars, ribbons, and more

EMMA HARDY

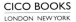

CICO BOOKS
LONDON NEW YORK

Published in 2008 by CICO Books
an imprint of Ryland Peters & Small
519 Broadway, 5th Floor, New York, NY 10012

www.cicobooks.com

10 9 8 7 6 5 4 3 2 1

A CIP catalog record for this book is available from the
Library of Congress.

ISBN-13: 978 1 906094 87 4

Printed in China

Editor: Marion Paull
Designer: Roger Hammond
Photographer: Debbie Patterson
Illustrator: Michael Hill
Templates: Anthony Duke

contents

introduction

Christmas wouldn't be Christmas without a beautifully decorated tree. The tradition dates back to the sixteenth century and originated in Germany, where trees were often decorated with paper flowers, nuts, and fruits.

Christmas trees were introduced to England in the 1840s when ornaments made of gingerbreads, and of wax, became popular, and the custom soon spread to America, brought by German settlers living in and around Pennsylvania. Candles were used to add sparkle until, in the 1890s, electric lights provided a much safer and troublefree way to illuminate the tree. The Victorians enjoyed decorating their trees with ornaments that were often home-made, including glass balls, small toys, beaded garlands, and sweets.

The idea of special tree top decorations may have originated with the creation of a gilded tin angel, sometime in the eighteenth century. The story goes that the daughter of a master craftsman died tragically, and appeared to her father in a dream, dressed in gold. So the next day, the craftsman made a tin doll clad in gold, and carved a wooden face to look like his beloved daughter. It being Christmas, his wife placed the angel on the top of their tree. The craftsman's friends encouraged him to make more angels and sell them at Christmas markets, and so started the tradition.

These days we have a wide and very varied selection of tree top decorations available to us, although the traditional angel is still very much a favorite. With this in mind, I have put together 25 projects using many different materials and styles. I hope that the tree top decorations you choose to make will become much-loved family heirlooms, ceremoniously unwrapped each year to take pride of place at the top of your tree, enjoyed and admired by all who see them.

the projects

From glittery angels and beautifully beaded snowflakes, to elegant foil flower bouquets and charming ribbon rosettes, there is a project here to suit every style and theme of tree. Each one is accompanied by illustrated instructions that will lead you step by step through the creative process, and photographs of the finished decoration show you what you are aiming for. A list of the materials used to create each one is provided, although you can make something unique by substituting items on the list for other materials.

None of the projects requires any complicated skills or knowledge and they can all be completed in a relatively short time. The finishing touches will make your decorations truly special, with beautiful buttons, beads, and ribbons adding the perfect final flourish.

glittery angel with wire wings

MATERIALS

Fine white tulle

Scissors, needle, and thread

Newspaper

Masking tape

Craft glue, bowl, and water

Gouache paints for skin and features, and paintbrush

30in. (75cm) length of dark brown ric rac

Small silver sequins

Thin wired garland, about 70in. (180cm)

Wired velvet ribbon

This glittery angel has a painted paper-mache head, but a large bead could be used to make it simpler. Delicate wings are made from fine garland to add sparkle—wired garland is best, so that the loops hold their shape.

1 Cut two layers of tulle measuring 43 x 7in. (110 x 18cm). Lay one on top of the other and sew running stitch about ½in. (1.5cm) from the top through both layers. Gently pull the thread to gather the material to make the dress. Finish with a few stitches to prevent the gathers pulling out.

2 Make the head by scrunching up newspaper, and secure with masking tape to hold the shape. Roll up a small piece of newspaper to make the neck and attach this to the head with masking tape. Then tear some more newspaper into small pieces. In a bowl, add water to craft glue to thin it a little, dip the torn pieces into it, and apply to the head and neck, covering them completely and ensuring that the surface is smooth. Leave to dry for several hours.

tip

Use gouache paints rather than poster paints for the angel's head because these are much easier to paint over if you need to cover a mistake. A final layer of paper varnish or undiluted craft glue gives a nice shiny finish, and also protects the paint.

3 Paint the head with flesh-colored paint and add eyes, nose, lips, and cheeks. Leave to dry. Cut five 6in. (15cm) lengths of ric rac for hair, and glue onto the head.

4 Apply glue around the neck and press the dress to it until it is firmly attached. Leave to dry. Glue little sequins around the bottom of the skirt.

5 Make five loops with the wire garland, using about 7in. (17cm) of garland for each one. Then make five smaller loops using about 4½in. (11cm) for each one. Fix the garland to the angel's back, leaving enough to twist around a branch to fasten the angel to the tree. Glue velvet ribbon around the neck. Then make a small garland tiara and glue in place.

paper-mache angel

MATERIALS

Paper for pattern and template on page 91

MATERIALS

Paper for pattern and template on page 91

White fabric

Pins and scissors

Needle and thread

Fiberfill

Newspaper

Craft glue, bowl, and water

White paint and paintbrush

Luster powder in white and copper/gold

Gouache paints for flesh, hair, and features

About 8in. (20cm) of thin gold ribbon

Silver wire for the tie

The smoothness of this charming angel comes from using small pieces of paper. Luster powders give a beautifully pearly finish but you can use ordinary gouache paint instead, and sprinkle fine glitter onto the surface while the paint is still wet.

1 Using the template on page 91, make paper patterns for the angel's body, wings, and arms. Fold the fabric in half, pin the pattern pieces in place and cut out two body pieces, two wing pieces, and two pieces for each arm.

2 With right sides facing, stitch together the body pieces, and then the wings and arms, leaving a small opening on each. Snip any curved seam allowances (to allow the material to lie flat), and turn the pieces right side out. Insert the fiberfill, pushing it into all corners, and hand stitch the openings closed.

3 In a bowl, add some water to the craft glue to thin it slightly. Tear newspaper into small pieces, dip these in the glue, and smooth them onto the padded shapes, using the smaller pieces around the edges and shaped areas. Apply two layers of newspaper and leave to dry overnight. Then paint the body, wings, and arms with white paint so that the newsprint does not show through. Leave to dry.

4 Mix the white luster powder with a little glue, paint onto the body and arms and leave to dry. Mix the copper/gold luster powder with some glue and paint onto the wings. Paint the hair, face and features, and hands with the gouache paints.

5 Tie gold ribbon round the angel's neck and glue the arms and wings in place. Twist silver wire around the middle of the wings to use to fasten the angel to the tree.

organza fairy

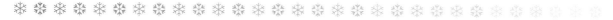

MATERIALS

Paper for the pattern and template on page 91

Pins and scissors

Needle and thread

Cream cotton fabric

Fiberfill

Metallic organza

Tacky glue

Fine sequins

Large shiny sequins

Embroidery floss in green, red, pink, and brown

30in. (75cm) length of 1½in. (4cm) wide organza ribbon

Glitter and glue

Scrap of ribbon for hair bow

16in. (40cm) length of ½in. (15mm) wide velvet ribbon

A beautiful ball gown covers this glamorous fairy's simple fabric body, and she is bedecked with sequins, large and small. A pretty shawl and little glitter shoes complete the look.

1 Using the templates on page 91, make paper patterns, pin to the cream cotton fabric and cut out two body shapes, four leg shapes, and four arm shapes. With right sides facing, machine stitch the arms and legs, leaving the tops open. Snip curved seams (to allow material to lie flat) and turn right way out.

Stitch the two body pieces together around the head and shoulders and down each side leaving the bottom open and a ³⁄₄in. (2cm) gap for each arm at either side. Stuff the arms and the legs.

2 Turn the body the right way out and push the arms in position, turning in ½in. (1cm) at each opening on the body. Stitch the arms in place and stuff the body. Tack the legs in position and stitch the bottom of the body closed.

3 Cut a 5 x 2¾in. (13 x 7cm) piece of organza. Fold lengthways and glue around the torso of the doll, holding in place until well fixed.

4 Cut two rectangles of organza 5½ x 17¾in. (14 x 45cm). Sew running stitch along the top edge of each piece and gather to form a skirt. Hold the gathers in place with a few stitches at the end. Glue one of the skirts in place on the doll. Then glue a line of small sequins along the bottom of the second skirt and when the glue is dry, glue this over the first skirt around the doll.

5 Glue shiny sequins around the waist and neckline of the dress, holding in place until securely fixed. Stitch two french knots on to the face for eyes in green embroidery floss, a small stitch of pink floss for the nose, and a few small stitches of red floss to form the mouth. Finish off the stitches at the back of the head.

6 Glue ½in. (1cm) lengths of brown embroidery floss to the head to form bangs. For the rest of the hair, cut longer lengths, about 3½in. (9cm), and glue them over the head from one side to the other. When the glue is dry, trim the hair to the required length. Glue a thin strip of sequins around the fairy's neck for a necklace.

7 With 16in. (40cm) of organza ribbon, make a loop, overlapping the ends of the ribbon slightly, and stitch together. Using running stitch, sew one side of the ribbon to the other to form two equal loops, and gather slightly. Do the same with a 14in. (35cm) length of ribbon. Stitch both pieces to the back of the fairy to form wings.

8 Cut a piece of organza 9 x 2in. (22 x 5cm) and glue sequins along both ends. Wrap this around the fairy's shoulders, like a shawl, and stitch in place. Paint glue on the end of the legs and sprinkle with glitter to make sparkly shoes. Leave to dry. Make a bow from a scrap of fabric and glue to the side of the head. Then sew the velvet ribbon to the fairy's back, just below the wings, to tie her to the tree.

knitted fairy

❋ ❋

MATERIALS

Knitting needles (size 3)

Pale pink yarn

Cream yarn

Needle and thread

Fiberfill

Yellow yarn

2 small blue beads

Pink embroidery floss

Silver embroidery floss

Silver ric rac

Fast-drying tacky glue

Silver ribbon

Thin ribbon

Only the most basic knowledge of knitting is necessary to make this cuddly fairy. Great for children, she would look lovely on a tree decorated with home-made woolly pompom ornaments.

1 Using pink yarn, cast on 20 stitches and knit stocking stitch for 20 rows. Change to cream wool and knit another 25 rows. Cast off.

2 Fold the knitted panel lengthways and, using cream wool, stitch up sides. With the seam at center back, sew running stitch around the top of the head section (pink) and gather. Finish with a few stitches to hold in place. Fill the knitted body with stuffing and stitch closed.

3 Tie a strand of pink yarn around the body, about 1½in. (4cm) from the top, and pull in gently to make the head. Knot at the back and trim the ends of the wool.

tip

This fairy sits well on a small tree. To make an angel for a bigger tree, increase the length of the skirt piece by adding on rows, keeping the head and arms the same size. For a fuller skirt, cast on more stitches to make the piece wider and gather up in the same way as step 5.

4 Stitch some lengths of yellow yarn to the top of the head to form the hair, sew on small beads for eyes, and sew a small mouth with pink embroidery floss.

5 Using the same knitting needles, and cream yarn, cast on 60 stitches and knit stocking stitch to a length of about 4in. (10cm). Cast off. Sew running stitch along the top of the knitting and gather to make the fairy's skirt. Embroider with stars, using the silver floss. Stitch the skirt on to the body and glue silver ric rac around the top. Glue a length of ric rac to the head to make a crown.

6 For the arms, cast on 8 stitches in cream yarn and knit a 4in. (10cm) panel in stocking stitch. Cast off. Using cream yarn, stitch the knitted panel lengthways to form a roll, and sew each end to either side of the body. Tie two pieces of silver ribbon into bows, one slightly bigger than the other, and sew to the back of the fairy, the bigger one on top, to make the wings. Then, under these, stitch a length of thin ribbon to make a tie.

ric rac fairy

✳ ✳

MATERIALS

Cream fabric for head

Green spotted fabric for body

Blue spotted fabric for skirt

Scissors

Needle and thread

Paper for pattern and template on page 92

Pins

Fiberfill

24in. (60cm) of ¼in. (8mm) wide gingham ribbon

14in. (35cm) blue ric rac

10in. (25cm) pink pompom fringe

Tacky glue

Blue and pink embroidery floss and needle

40in. (1 meter) gold ric rac for hair

Scrap of white ric rac for crown

Button for crown and two for feet

Perfect for a less formal tree, this cute fairy is made from scraps of fabric and buttons. Stitch the body and then raid your workbox for bits of ric rac, braid, and buttons to decorate her. Gingham ribbon stitched to her back forms her wings when tied to the tree.

1 Cut a piece of cream fabric measuring 2¼ x 10¼in. (6 x 26cm), a piece of body fabric 3½ x 10¼in. (9 x 26cm), and a piece of skirt fabric 3¾ x 10¼in. (9.5 x 26cm). With right sides facing, sew the long sides of the cream fabric and body fabric together, and then the long sides of the body and skirt fabric. Press the seams open.

2 Cut out a paper pattern for the fairy using the template on page 92. Fold the fabric panel in half and lay the paper pattern across it as shown. Pin and cut out.

tip

To simplify this fairy, cut out the front and
back from one piece of fabric rather than
joining bands of different fabrics as here.
Make the face with buttons so that the
features stand out.

3 With right sides facing, pin and stitch the two pieces together, leaving the bottom open. Turn right side out and fill with fiberfill. Turn in the raw bottom edge by ½in. (1.5cm). Cut two pieces of gingham ribbon, each 2in. (5cm) long, position them inside the bottom open edge to form legs and tack in place. Then stitch along the bottom.

4 Glue ric rac around the neck and waist of the fairy, overlapping the ends at the back, and then glue a length of pompom fringe around the bottom, again overlapping the ends at the back.

5 Embroider two blue French knots on the face for eyes and make a few small pink stitches to form the mouth. Finish with a few stitches at the back of the head. Cut eight 5in. (12.5cm) lengths of gold ric rac and glue around the head to make the hair.

6 Glue a piece of ric rac on to the head to make a crown and decorate with a button glued to the middle. Glue a button on to each leg. Stitch a length of gingham ribbon to the back of the fairy, at its center, and tie to the tree with a large bow to form the wings.

peg-doll fairy

MATERIALS

Round wooden clothespin

Selection of gouache paints for the skin, hair, and features

Paintbrush

Gold organza

Scissors, needle, and thread

Fast-drying, tacky craft glue

24in. (60cm) of 1½in. (35mm) wide gold organza ribbon

Flower sequin for hair

Star sequin and string of tiny sequins for the wand

Gold sequins

Ribbon about 16in. (40cm) long

Add a touch of sophistication to your tree with this beautiful Christmas fairy. No one will guess that she is made from a plain, old-fashioned wooden clothespin "dressed" with organza and sequins.

1 Paint the peg with flesh-colored paint. When dry, paint the hair and facial features. Again leave to dry.

2 Cut two pieces of organza, each measuring 9 x 4in. (22 x 10cm). Lay one piece on top of the other and, close to the top edge, sew running stitch through both layers. Pull the thread to gather the material, making sure that it fits around the clothespin. Finish with a few stitches to hold the gathers.

tip

If you cannot find a flower sequin for the fairy's hair decoration, glue a tiny ribbon bow in place instead, or a cluster of tiny beads in a flower shape.

3 Position the skirt around the peg and stitch together at the back. Apply a dab of glue to the clothespn and skirt to hold in place if necessary.

4 Fold the gold ribbon in half lengthways. Dab glue around the body of the clothespin and wrap the ribbon around it, tying it at the back. Leave to dry. Open out the remaining ribbon and trim the ends in a V shape.

5 Tie the ribbon in an extravagant bow. Glue a flower sequin to the hair. Make a wand from string sequins and a star sequin, and glue in place. Glue gold sequins on to the skirt. Stitch a ribbon to the back of the fairy for the tie.

button snowflake

❄ ❄

MATERIALS

2 buttons about 1in. (30mm) in diameter

16 buttons about 9/10in. (22mm) in diameter

16 buttons about 4/5in. (20mm) in diameter

24 buttons about 7/10in. (17mm) in diameter

16 buttons about 3/5in. (15mm) in diameter

16 buttons about 1/2in. (12mm) in diameter

16 buttons about 1/4in. (7mm) in diameter

Glue gun and glue sticks

4 lengths of floral wire, each about 10in. (25cm)

Nipper for wire

Scrap paper and pencil

Ruler

16in. (40cm) of 1/2in. (10mm) wide ribbon

Craft knife

Create a beautiful and everlasting decoration for your tree with this unusual snowflake. Mother-of-pearl buttons add an extra special touch but any buttons can be used.

1 Arrange the buttons in order of size. Lay one of the large buttons wrong side up on the work surface and apply a blob of glue just above and just below the holes. This will reduce the amount of glue that oozes through to the front of the button. Press a length of wire on to it so that the button is placed centrally. Stick the next size of button directly above the central button, touching the edges.

Again, try to apply the glue to either side of the holes. Continue with five more buttons, decreasing in size, and repeat on the other side of the central button.

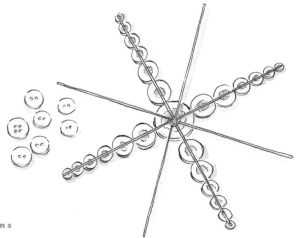

2 Cut another length of wire in half and glue each piece to the central button to form a cross with the first wire. Glue on buttons as before. Lay the cross of buttons face down on a piece of scrap paper, and draw lines to make a star shape. Cut the remaining two lengths of wire in half.

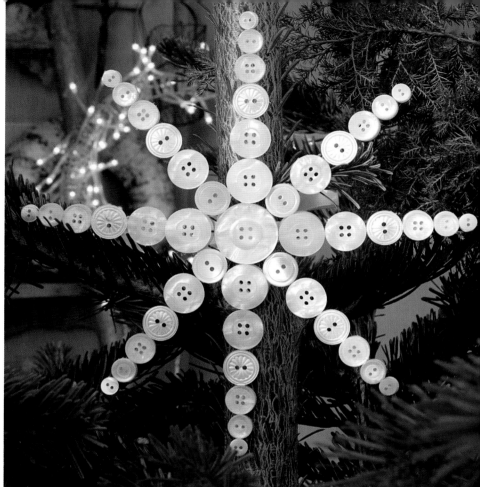

3 Using the drawn lines as guides, lay ⁷⁄₁₀in. (17mm) buttons next to the central button, in the gaps. Then, continue along each drawn arm, first with a slightly bigger button followed by smaller ones, decreasing in size as before. Glue the wires to the backs of the buttons, and to the central button. Then glue all the corresponding buttons on to the backs of the snowflake buttons except for the central button.

4 Lay the ribbon across the back of the star, make sure it's taut and flat, and glue to the central button. Glue the remaining big button in place. To remove any excess glue from the buttons, carefully scrape off with a craft knife making sure that the buttons themselves do not get scratched.

pearl bead snowflake

MATERIALS

Silver jeweler's wire

Pliers

Selection of pearly beads

Glue gun and glue sticks

Length of floral wire

This charming snowflake is so beautiful it may well become a family heirloom. Beads in lovely pearly colors are threaded onto stiff wire and glued in place.

1 Cut three lengths of silver jeweler's wire, each measuring 12in. (30cm). Thread five beads of varying sizes onto each one and thread the same pattern of beads in reverse on the other end.

2 Cut another three lengths, this time 6in. (15cm) long, and twist each one to the existing arms between the second and third beads. Thread five beads onto each side of these short arms and bend the ends of the wires over the end beads, trimming if necessary. Apply a small dab of glue to the main arm's last bead and wire.

3 Lay the three long beaded lengths on top of each other and twist them together at the center to hold them in place.

tip
If using large beads,
the snowflake may
become quite heavy
and will be more suited
to a larger tree that will
support the weight.

4 Cut three more lengths of wire and twist them onto the other ends of the main arms, threading five beads as before and bending the ends of the wire over the final bead.

5 Glue a small bead onto the ends of all six main arms, snipping the wires if they are too long.

6 Twist a length of thick floral wire around the center of the snowflake and push to the back to attach to the top of the tree. With the glue gun, glue a bead to the center of the snowflake to finish it.

clear seed bead snowflake

MATERIALS

Silver jeweler's wire

Pliers

Clear seed beads

Clear bugle beads

This delicate snowflake will add subtle elegance to your festive decorations. Clear beads catch the light beautifully, so drape fairy lights around the top of the tree to make the snowflake glisten.

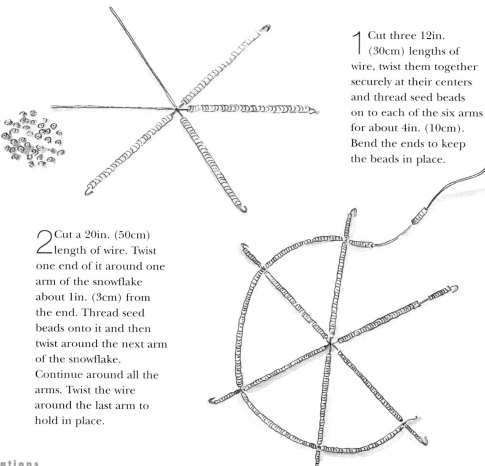

1 Cut three 12in. (30cm) lengths of wire, twist them together securely at their centers and thread seed beads on to each of the six arms for about 4in. (10cm). Bend the ends to keep the beads in place.

2 Cut a 20in. (50cm) length of wire. Twist one end of it around one arm of the snowflake about 1in. (3cm) from the end. Thread seed beads onto it and then twist around the next arm of the snowflake. Continue around all the arms. Twist the wire around the last arm to hold in place.

3 Cut six 6in. (15cm) lengths of wire. Take one and twist one end to an arm just above the circle of beads and thread on three bugle beads, then seven seed beads and another three bugle beads and form a petal shape. Twist the wire around the main arm and repeat to make another petal on the other side. Twist around the main arm again and trim. Repeat on each arm of the snowflake.

4 Cut a 47in. (120cm) length of wire. Twist one end of it onto a main arm about 3in. (8cm) from the end. Thread on six bugle beads and twist around the next arm. When the circle is complete, thread two bugle beads on to the wire, three seed beads and another two bugle beads, and twist around the main arm. Thread on three bugle beads, seven seed beads, and another three bugle beads and form a petal shape. Twist around the wire circle and thread two bugle, three seed, and two bugle beads, forming another petal. Repeat all the way round.

5 For the flower shape at the center of the snowflake, cut six lengths of wire. On each one, thread three bugle beads, seven seed beads, and another three bugle beads and twist the wire ends around the center.

6 Cut another six lengths of wire and thread with two bugle beads, seven seed beads, and another two bugle beads. Twist these on to the outer circle of the snowflake, one in each section. Twist more wire around the center a couple of times to attach the snowflake to the tree.

pipe cleaner snowflake

MATERIALS

14 white pipe cleaners, each 12in. (30cm) long

Scissors

Silver jeweler's wire

Newspaper

Spray adhesive

White glitter

With a few twists and turns, this crisp snowflake takes shape. Finished with a light sprinkle of white glitter to create a subtle shimmer, it stands out against the background of a Christmas tree.

1 Using four of the pipe cleaners, twist each end to form a loop about ¾in. (2cm) long, bending the end of the wire round the main stem to hold in place.

2 Take another pipe cleaner and twist the end underneath the loop of one of the pipe cleaners from step 1 to form a loop at each side. Bend the pipe cleaner round the main stem and make another two loops underneath the first, finishing by twisting the pipe cleaner round the main stem and trimming off any excess with a pair of scissors. Repeat at the ends of all four pipe cleaners.

3 Cut eight pieces of pipe cleaner measuring 2¾in. (7cm). Twist them on to each pipe cleaner about 3in. (8cm) from the end and form into V shapes.

4 Lay the four pipe cleaners across each other to make a snowflake shape. Cut a piece of wire about 8in. (20cm) long and bind around the center of the snowflake to hold all the pipe cleaners together. The end of the wire should be at the back of the snowflake, so that it can be used as a tie. In a well-ventilated area, and having covered the work surface with newspaper, spray the snowflake with spray adhesive, sprinkle it with white glitter and shake off any excess.

shiny bead snowflake

MATERIALS

Silver jeweler's wire

Selection of metallic and pearly beads

Pliers

Metallic beads have a delightfully frosted look that works perfectly for this stylish decoration. The beads are threaded onto wire with smaller "arms" added to make the shape of the snowflake, using beads in shades of green and silver.

1 Cut three lengths of wire, each measuring 12in. (30cm). Thread beads onto each wire for about 4in. (10cm), starting with four small ones. Then thread on the same pattern of beads in reverse. Bend the ends of the wire slightly to keep the beads in place. Leave some space between the beads at this stage.

2 Lay the three beaded wires on top of each other to form a star shape and twist them together at their centers to hold them in place.

3 Cut another three lengths of wire measuring 6in. (15cm). Thread beads on to them as before, this time for about 2in. (5cm), and again repeat the bead pattern in reverse, leaving some space between the beads and bending over the ends of the wire slightly. Twist the short lengths of beaded wire evenly around the center of the star shape.

tip

Before you start, make
sure the wire is narrow
enough to thread through
the beads.

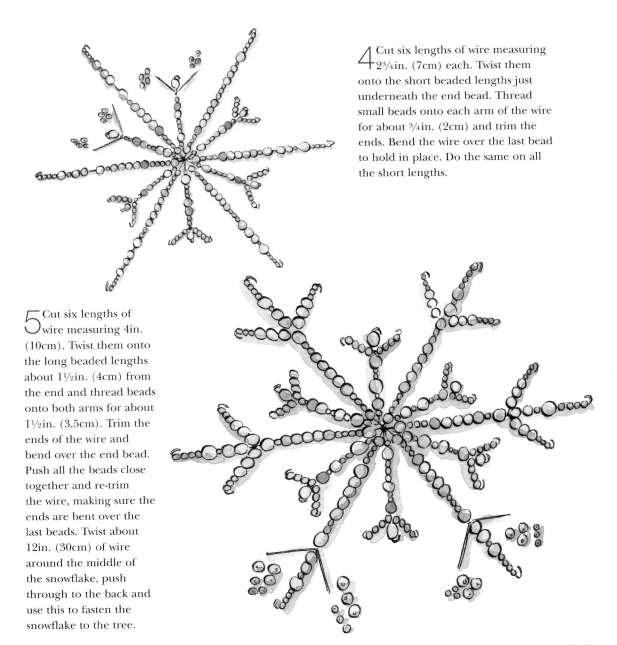

4 Cut six lengths of wire measuring 2¾in. (7cm) each. Twist them onto the short beaded lengths just underneath the end bead. Thread small beads onto each arm of the wire for about ¾in. (2cm) and trim the ends. Bend the wire over the last bead to hold in place. Do the same on all the short lengths.

5 Cut six lengths of wire measuring 4in. (10cm). Twist them onto the long beaded lengths about 1½in. (4cm) from the end and thread beads onto both arms for about 1½in. (3.5cm). Trim the ends of the wire and bend over the end bead. Push all the beads close together and re-trim the wire, making sure the ends are bent over the last beads. Twist about 12in. (30cm) of wire around the middle of the snowflake, push through to the back and use this to fasten the snowflake to the tree.

pinecone star

❋ ❋

MATERIALS

1 large pinecone

18 small pinecones

Floral wire and pliers

Craft glue and paintbrush

Newspaper

White glitter

Take inspiration from nature with this lovely star. A light dusting of glitter gives the cones a beautiful frosted finish.

1 Take a length of wire and push through the lower part of a small pinecone. Twist the wire round it to hold securely. Add another pinecone, twisting the wire around it again, and then add a third. Make six of these three-cone wires.

2 Push the ends of the wires through the lower section of the large pinecone and twist round to hold each arm in place, arranging them evenly.

3 Paint craft glue on to the pinecones, dabbing it roughly over them. Lay the star on newspaper and sprinkle glitter all over it. Shake off any excess and leave to dry.

4 Twist a length of wire around the underside of the large pinecone, fastening it securely to attach the star to the tree top.

tip

This star is very
economical to make if
you gather the pinecones
from parks and woods,
where they have fallen
from the trees.

glitter star

✳ ✳

MATERIALS

Paper for pattern and templates on page 93

Thin card

Pencil, ruler, and craft knife

Cutting mat or scrap paper

Craft glue

Glitter

Cardboard cut into a star shape, scored with a craft knife and then gently folded creates a simple 3-D decoration. Cover it with fine glitter for a stylish tree topper.

1 Using the template on page 93, a pencil, ruler, and craft knife, draw and cut out a star shape from thin card. A cutting mat or pile of scrap paper will protect the work surface.

2 Score lines from point to point on the star by gently pulling the craft knife along the edge of the ruler to cut just the surface of the card. Do not press too hard or the knife will cut through the card. Follow all the lines as indicated on the template, and gently bend the card to give it shape.

3 Using the other template, cut out a piece of card for the base and roll it into a cone shape. Glue the edges together, holding it in place until the glue has dried slightly.

4 Paint the star and base with glue, ensuring an even finish. Sprinkle glitter all over it and shake gently to remove any excess. Leave to dry.

tip

Glitter is available in lots of different colors so your star doesn't have to be silver. Make a star using colored glitter to co-ordinate with the other decorations.

organza star

✳ ✳

MATERIALS

Organza

Needle and thread

Fiberfill

Tacky glue

String of sequins

Little sparkly jewels

Gold ric rac

Wide organza ribbon

This bejewelled fabric star will take pride of place at the top of the Christmas tree. Tie it on with a sumptuous bow, ensuring the sparkly star looks equally lovely from front and back.

1 Using the template on page 93, cut out two stars from organza. With wrong sides facing, sew the two together with running stitch all the way round, leaving an opening along one point of the star.

2 Fill the star with fiberfill, making sure that the fiberfill is pushed into the points and there are no lumps. Stitch the opening closed.

3 Apply a thin line of glue all round the star close to the edge and press sequins to it. Overlap the ends slightly and leave the glue to dry for a few minutes.

4 Decorate the star by applying small dabs of glue to it and carefully sticking on little sparkly jewels.

5 Apply glue all round the edge of the star and run ric rac along it, holding it in place until it is fixed. Overlap the ends slightly.

6 Cut a length of organza ribbon long enough to tie in a bow and stitch it to the back of the star. Use this to tie the star to the tree.

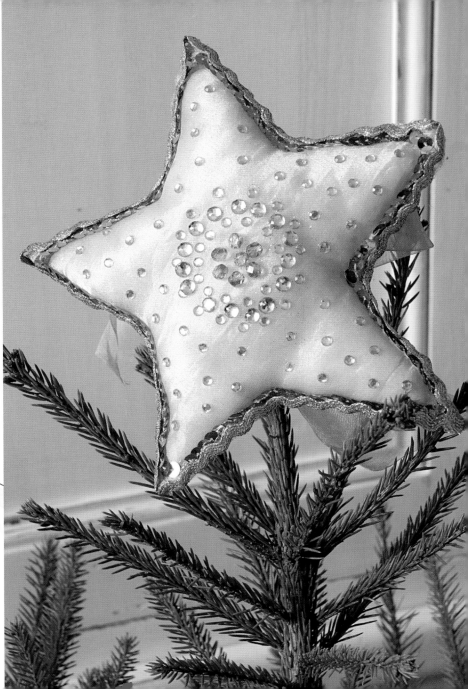

ribbon poinsettia

❉ ✳ ❉ ✳ ❉ ✳ ❉ ✳ ❉ ✳ ❉ ✳ ❉ ✳ ❉ ✳ ❉ ✳ ❉ ✳ ❉ ✳ ❉ ✳ ❉ ✳ ❉ ✳ ❉ ✳ ❉ ✳

MATERIALS

43in. (110cm) of 2½in. (6.5cm) wide red wired taffeta ribbon

30in. (75cm) of 2½in. (6.5cm) green wired taffeta ribbon

8in. (20cm) of 1in. (2.5cm) wide red wired taffeta ribbon

Scissors, needle, and thread

Green metallic beads

16in. (40cm) of ¾in. (22mm) wide red satin ribbon

This red flower is the perfect tree-top decoration. Wired ribbon holds its shape, and taffeta gives a lovely sheen.

1 Cut six 3½in. (9cm) lengths of the wide red ribbon. Sew small running stitches at both ends of each strip and pull up so that the ribbon is gathered, securing it with a few stitches. Stitch the ends of three petals together and then do the same with the other three. Stitch the two sets of three together at the center to form an even flower. Then cut six 3in. (8cm) lengths of the same wide red ribbon and repeat to make a slightly smaller flower.

2 Cut four 4in. (10cm) lengths of green ribbon, sew running stitches at one end of each and gather as before. Cut the other end of each strip into a leaf shape.

3 Stitch the leaves to the back of the smaller flower at regular intervals. Then stitch the large flower to the back of this. Cut a 12in. (30cm) length of green ribbon, fold it in half and stitch to the back of the flower, cutting a neat V shape in both ends.

4 Cut two lengths of the
thinner taffeta ribbon and
sew a few stitches in the center
of each one to gather them
slightly. Cut the ends into
petal shapes and stitch the
ribbon petals crossways in the
middle of the flower. Finish
with a few beads at the center.
Stitch a length of satin ribbon
to the back of the flower to
make a tie, and if necessary,
adjust the petals and leaves to
sit evenly.

patterned fabric flower

MATERIALS

3 different patterns of red fabrics

Paper for pattern and template on page 90

Self-covering button with spotty fabric

16in. (40cm) of red ribbon

Go dotty for this cute spotty flower. Polka-dot fabric with its endearingly retro feel creates a jolly bloom, but any fabric could be used. Co-ordinate other tree decorations to match, choosing strong shapes in keeping with the tree topper.

1 Using the template on page 90, cut out patterns for the two sizes of petals. Then cut out two times eight of the bigger petals in the same fabric. With right sides facing, pin and machine stitch each one, leaving the end open. Make small snips round the seam allowance (so that the material lies flat), turn right side out and press. Using the smaller petal pattern, make three petals as before in each of the other two fabrics, and press.

2 Gather the open end of each of the bigger petals slightly and hold in place with a few stitches. Then stitch the petals together to form a flower.

3 Repeat step 2 using the smaller petals, alternating the two fabric patterns. Stitch to the middle of the big flower and sew the button to the center.

4 Stitch the ribbon to the back of the flower securely to make the tie.

metallic foil flowers tied in a bunch

MATERIALS

Paper for pattern and templates on page 92

Metallic foil

Scissors

Scrap paper

Ballpoint pen

Pin

Thin silver wire

Pliers

Small metallic beads

Glue gun and sticks

16in. (40cm) of wired ribbon

This bouquet adds a subtle, elegant charm to your tree. The sparkling metallic flowers are arranged by bending the silver-wire stems to make a stunning display.

1 Using the templates on page 92, make two paper patterns for the flowers and cut out six large and four small flowers from the foil.

2 Place the foil flowers on a pile of scrap paper and, using the ballpoint pen, make small dots all the way round the petals, a line from the center along each petal, and a few dots around the middle.

3 Using a pin, make a small hole at the center of each flower. Cut about 10in. (25cm) of silver wire and push this through the hole from back to front. Thread a bead onto the wire and push the wire back through the hole.

tip

Metallic foils are available in copper and
gold as well as silver. Flowers in these
lovely finishes would make a very pretty
display. Alternatively, glass paint, which
is available in a wide selection of hues,
can be applied to silver foil to create
flowers in all sorts of colors for a
beautifully bright bouquet.

4 Twist the wire around itself at the back of the flower. Apply a little glue to the back of the flower, using the glue gun, and stick the wire down.

6 Tie the ribbon around the bunch and to the top of the tree, finishing with a neat bow. Trim the ends of the ribbon if necessary.

5 When all the flowers have been wired, make a bunch and twist the wires together to hold in place. Trim the ends of the wire so that they are all the same length.

beaded berries

❄❄❄❄❄❄❄❄❄❄❄❄❄❄❄❄❄❄❄❄❄❄❄❄❄❄❄❄❄❄❄

MATERIALS

Green jeweler's wire

Red seed beads

Green seed beads

Tacky glue

12 beads for the berries

Length of floral wire

Wire cutters

Ribbon

Red berries are a traditional motif at Christmas time, and these beautiful beaded berries, gathered in a leafy cluster and tied onto the tree, will keep their shape and color perfectly throughout the holiday season.

1 Cut a 8in. (20cm) length of jeweler's wire and thread a bead on to the end of it. Bend the wire over the bead and twist the end back on itself to hold it in place. Paint the bead with glue and sprinkle red seed beads onto it to cover it completely. Make 12 of these.

3 Continue to wire the beaded berries onto the main stem, varying the angles and making the stems of the berries gradually longer towards the bottom.

2 Take a length of floral wire and start to twist the berry stems onto it, making sure that they are firmly held in place. Snip off any excess wire.

4 Cut a 6in. (15cm) length of green wire and thread green seed beads onto the end. Bend the beaded section into a leaf shape and then twist the end of it around the rest of the wire at the base of the leaf to keep the beads in place. Make several of these leaves.

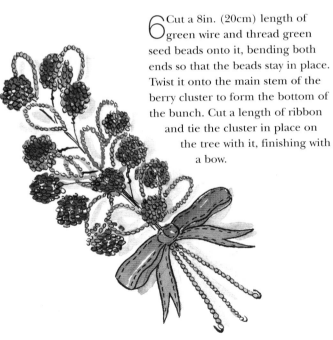

6 Cut a 8in. (20cm) length of green wire and thread green seed beads onto it, bending both ends so that the beads stay in place. Twist it onto the main stem of the berry cluster to form the bottom of the bunch. Cut a length of ribbon and tie the cluster in place on the tree with it, finishing with a bow.

5 Attach the leaves to the berry cluster by twisting the ends onto the main stem as before. Vary the angles of the leaves and twist the stems around until you are happy with the arrangement.

glitter bird

✻ ✻

MATERIALS

Paper for pattern and template on page 90

10in. (25cm) length of 53in. (135cm) wide velvet fabric

Pins

Scissors

Needle and thread

Feathers

Fiberfill

Seed beads

Sequins

Flower sequin

Bugle beads

20in. (50cm) of ½in. (15mm) wide velvet ribbon

A sparkling blue velvet bird with a delicate feathery tail and sequinned wings looks fabulous perched on the top of a traditional Christmas tree, or clipped to your own resplendent arrangement of branches and twigs.

1 Make a paper pattern using the template on page 90, pin to the velvet fabric, and cut out two pieces for the bird's body, one piece for the base and two wing pieces.

2 With right sides facing, pin and stitch the two body pieces together, leaving a gap of 4¾in. (12cm) at the bottom and a gap at the tail.

3 Pin the base piece along the opening at the bottom of the bird, leaving a gap of about 1½in. (4cm) along one side. Turn right side out.

4 Turn in the raw edge at the tail by ½in. (1.5cm) and push the base of the feathers into it. Hand stitch securely in place.

5 Fill the bird with small pieces of fiberfill, pushing them through the opening right into the beak and tail shape. Make sure that there are no lumps and when the bird is full, hand stitch the opening closed.

6 Hand stitch seed beads to the beak and under the tail feathers. Sew sequins randomly over the bird and use a flower sequin and three seed beads to make an eye.

7 Take the two velvet wing pieces and, right sides facing, pin and stitch them together, leaving an opening of about 1in. (2.5cm) along one edge. Snip around the seam allowance and turn right side out. Hand stitch the opening closed and press.

8 Decorate the wings with bugle beads and seed beads and hand stitch them onto the body of the bird. Stitch the velvet ribbon to the back of the bird securely to make the tie.

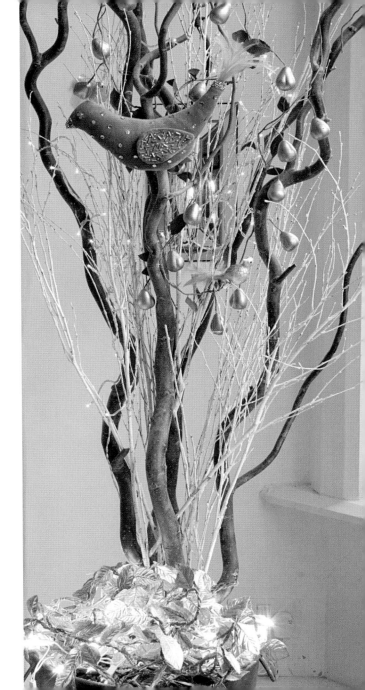

organza butterfly

❋ ❋

MATERIALS

20in. (50cm) of silver jeweler's wire

Small silver beads

10 beads about ¼in. (7mm) wide

4 glass beads for antennas

Pliers

Scissors, needle, and thread

Copper-colored organza 10in. (25cm)

String sequins 40in. (1 metre)

String of small sequins 20in. (50cm)

Selection of sequins

Tacky glue

16in. (40cm) of 1½in. (36mm) wide gold organza ribbon

This delicate butterfly looks as though it has just landed on the tree. Its body and antennas are beaded while its wings are strips of shimmery organza. Make smaller butterflies in the same way to decorate the rest of the tree, adding sequins for extra twinkle.

1 Fold the wire in two and thread one small silver bead onto it, pushing the bead to the bend. Thread the other beads onto the two strands of wire together, alternating between small silver beads and larger ones.

2 Pull the ends of the wire slightly apart to form antennas, and thread a glass bead onto each one. Follow these with 12 small silver beads and finish with another glass bead on both pieces of wire. Trim the wire and bend the end over the glass bead to hold securely in place.

3 Cut a piece of organza measuring 17¾ x 4in. (45 x 10cm). Fray the edges. Fold the strip in half lengthways. Overlap the ends slightly and join one side to the other in the middle, using running stitch through all the layers. Pull the thread to gather and secure with a few stitches.

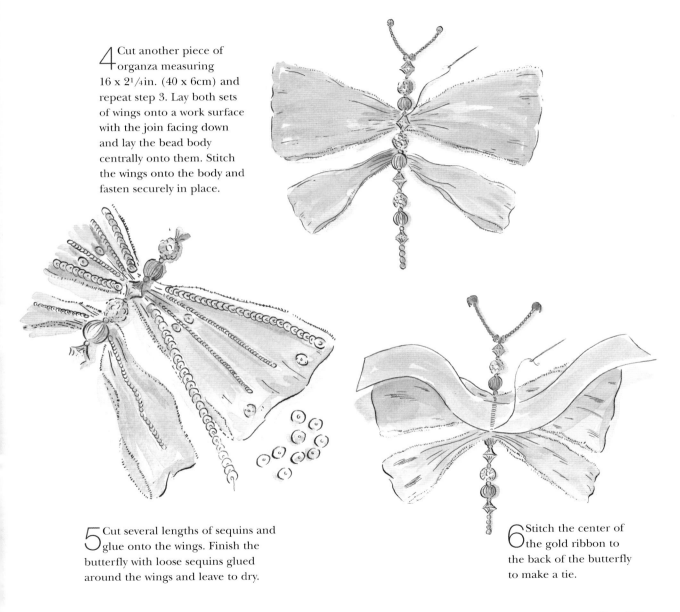

4 Cut another piece of organza measuring 16 x 2¼in. (40 x 6cm) and repeat step 3. Lay both sets of wings onto a work surface with the join facing down and lay the bead body centrally onto them. Stitch the wings onto the body and fasten securely in place.

5 Cut several lengths of sequins and glue onto the wings. Finish the butterfly with loose sequins glued around the wings and leave to dry.

6 Stitch the center of the gold ribbon to the back of the butterfly to make a tie.

grosgrain ribbon rosette

MATERIALS

41½ x 3in. (105 x 8cm) grosgrain ribbon, salmon pink

Needle and thread

Tacky glue

22 x 2in. (56 x 5cm) grosgrain ribbon, shocking pink

35½ x 1in. (90 x 2.5cm) grosgrain ribbon, orange

1¼in. (30mm) button

Make a statement with this bold, contemporary ribbon rosette. Grosgrain ribbon holds its shape very well and falls easily into neat folds, so is perfect for making this striking tree decoration.

1 Take the salmon pink ribbon and fold it approximately every 2in. (5cm) into an accordion, finishing with both ends facing the same way. Hold the folded ribbon firmly as you go.

2 Carefully push a needle and thread through all the layers of ribbon, centrally and about ¼in. (5mm) from the bottom edge. You may need to separate the layers slightly with your fingers and push the needle through a few layers at a time. Tie the ends of the thread together in front of the raw edges. Knot firmly, close to the ribbon.

3 Apply a line of glue along one raw edge and press against the other raw edge, holding them together until they are firmly stuck.

4 Flatten out the rosette, so that the folds are even. Repeat this process with the shocking pink ribbon, folding it about every 1¼in. (3cm), and then with 16in. (40cm) of the orange ribbon, folding it every 1in. (2.5cm). Position the shocking pink rosette centrally on the salmon pink rosette and the orange rosette centrally on these two. Stitch them all in place and sew a button securely to the center of the rosette. The remaining orange ribbon can be used for the tie. Lay it across the back of the rosette so that an equal length extends each side and stitch it on securely.

taffeta ribbon bow

❄ ✻ ❄ ✻ ❄ ✻ ❄ ✻ ❄ ✻ ❄ ✻ ❄ ✻ ❄ ✻ ❄ ✻ ❄ ✻ ❄ ✻ ❄ ✻ ❄ ✻ ❄ ✻ ❄ ✻

MATERIALS

102 x 2in. (260 x 5cm) wired taffeta ribbon

Scissors, needle and thread

1in. (30mm) self-covering button

16 x ½in. (40 x 1cm) satin ribbon for the tie

Presents aren't the only things that can be decorated with a ribbon bow. This smart rosette is made with wired taffeta ribbon fashioned into loops, which can be arranged evenly on the tree.

1 Cut four 17¾in. (45cm) lengths of taffeta ribbon. Form a loop with each piece of ribbon, overlapping the ends by 3cm (1in.). Stitch in place.

2 For each one, flatten the loop, with the join in the middle, and stitch through the layers, pulling the thread to gather the ribbon slightly. With the joins at the back, lay one ribbon loop diagonally across another one, stitching them through the center to hold the two together. Lay the remaining two loops across diagonally to complete the flower shape, and again stitch each one at the center to hold in place.

3 Cut a 12in. (30cm) length of the same ribbon. Sew running stitch along one edge and pull the thread to gather the ribbon into a rosette. Finish with a few stitches to secure. Cover a button with a piece of the ribbon, stitch it centrally onto the rosette, and then sew this at the center of the ribbon flower.

4 Cut approximately 16in. (40cm) of the same ribbon and fold in half widthways. Stitch it to the back of the decoration, leaving the ends hanging down, and trim the ends into a V shape. Sew on the satin ribbon just above this to form the tie.

foil heart

MATERIALS

Paper for pattern,
template on page 92
and pencil

Metallic foil

Masking tape

Pile of scrap paper

Ballpoint pen

Scissors

Rolling pin

Tacky glue

Metallic foil is soft, pliable and easy to work with, so this striking heart decoration is simplicity itself to make, even with its intricate pattern of stars and dainty border.

1 Using the template on page 92, make a paper pattern, and draw the design on it. Stick this to the foil, using small pieces of masking tape to hold it in place.

2 Lay the foil on a pile of scrap paper with the pattern face up. Draw over the design with the pen, pressing firmly to transfer the pattern to the foil.

tip

Why not decorate the tree with some small
hearts, too? Make them in the same way
as the tree top heart. Use a hole punch to
make a hole at the top of each one, and
hang them on to the branches with lengths
of thin ribbon.

3 Cut out the heart shape from the foil (carefully because the edges of the foil can be sharp.) Remove the paper pattern. Go over any areas of pattern that may need it.

4 Lay the cut-out foil on a work surface and roll over it with a rolling pin to flatten it out.

5 Cut an 3 x 4¾in. (8 x 12cm) piece of foil and make this into a roll, using the longer side as the height of the roll. Overlap the edges by about ¾in. (2cm) and glue in place. When the glue is dry, stick the roll to the back of the heart and again leave to dry. This tube will slot over the top branch of the tree and keep the heart in place.

christmas ball wreath

❄ ❄

MATERIALS

Silver wire and cutters

Approximately 55 small Christmas balls between ³/₄in. (2cm) and 1in. (2.5cm) wide in pinks and silver

26 x 1¹/₄in. (65 x 3cm) silver ribbon

Scissors

Wreaths are traditional Christmas decorations so why not use one on the top of the tree? Look for miniature Christmas balls and wire them together to make a mini wreath, finishing it with a ribbon bow.

1 Cut a 59in. (150cm) length of wire. Make a circle with the wire about 5in. (13cm) in diameter, bending it around itself so that it's solid. Then cut as many small pieces of wire as there are balls. Make them about 4in. (10cm) long, and thread each one through a ball, twisting the wire firmly.

2 Attach the balls to the wire circle, winding the wire around to hold the balls in place securely. Try to avoid using two balls of the same color next to each other. Continue attaching balls to the wire circle until the whole wreath base is covered. Move the balls if necessary to create an even look.

3 Cut a 14in. (35cm) length of ribbon, and then cut a piece of wire 6in. (15cm) long and twist it around the middle of the ribbon. Push the ends of the wire through the wreath, from the front, and twist to hold it in place at the back.

4 Tie the ribbon in a neat bow and trim the ends at an angle. Tie the rest of the ribbon to the back of the wreath at the top and fasten with a knot. Use this to tie the bauble wreath to the tree.

salt-dough gingerbread man

Make a gingerbread man that looks good enough to eat. Baked hard and then painted, the figure is finished with buttons and ric rac glued around the edge to look like icing.

MATERIALS

Mixing bowl, wooden spoon, measuring cup

5oz (150g) salt

3½ fl. oz (100ml) lukewarm water

5oz (150g) flour

½ tablespoon vegetable oil

Rolling pin

Gingerbread cookie cutter

Baking tray

Brown gouache paint and paintbrush

40in. (1 metre) white ric rac

Tacky glue

2 black buttons

3 white buttons

Small piece of red felt for mouth

10in. (25cm) gingham ribbon for bow

20in. (50cm) ribbon for ties

Strong glue

1 Mix together the salt and water in a bowl, dissolving as much of the salt as possible. Add the flour and oil and mix together to form a pliable dough. Add more water or flour if necessary.

2 Sprinkle flour onto the work surface and roll the dough out to a thickness of about ½in. (1.5cm). Cut the gingerbread man using the cutter and place on the baking tray. Bake in the oven heated to 200F for about an hour. Check the dough to see if it is hard. It may need slightly longer—if so, leave in the oven and check regularly. When it's ready, turn off the heat and leave the gingerbread man to cool in the oven to reduce the risk of cracking.

tip

Salt dough is very easy to make and use, but needs to be "cooked" on a very low temperature so that it does not crack. Leave the salt dough figure in the oven to go completely cold when the oven is turned off to prevent cracking as it cools

3 Paint the figure with brown paint and leave to dry. Paint both sides of the figure ensuring even coverage.

4 Using the tacky glue, stick ric rac all the way round the gingerbread man, overlapping the ends slightly. For a neat finish, hold the ric rac in place at corners and curved areas until the glue is dry.

5 Glue on black button eyes and red fabric mouth. Stick three white buttons to the middle of the figure, and a gingham bow at the neck. Leave the glue to dry completely.

6 Cut two pieces of ribbon, each about 10in. (25cm) long, and use the strong glue to stick them to the back of the gingerbread man, one at the top of the body and the second one slightly lower down. This ensures that the gingerbread man will sit securely at the top of the tree.

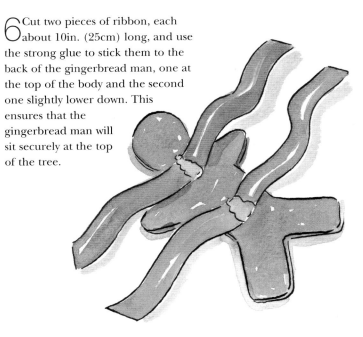

templates

❋ ❋

glitter bird p68

patterned
flower petals
p58

paper-mache angel
wings and arms p14

organza fairy p18

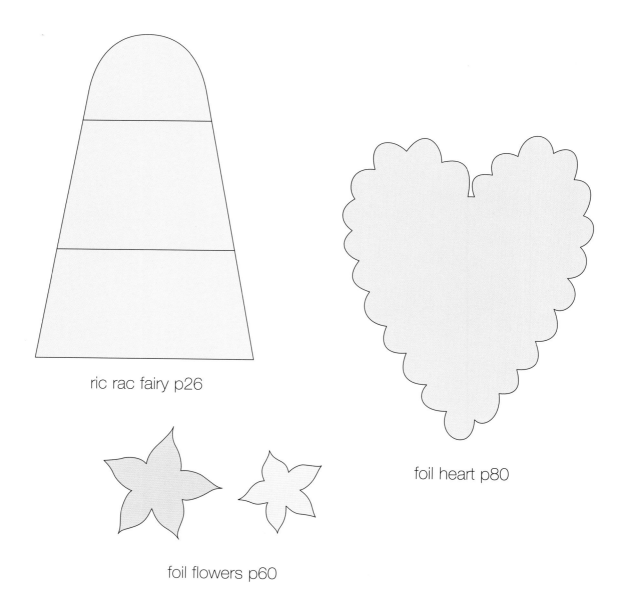

ric rac fairy p26

foil heart p80

foil flowers p60

glitter star p52

glitter star p52

Organza star p54

stockists

Amy Butler
For Stockists see
www.amybutlerdesigns.com

Art Supplies Online
800-967-7367
www.artsuppliesonline.com

Britex Fabrics
146 Geary Street
San Francisco
CA 94108
415-392-2910
www.britexfabrics.com

Crafts etc.
800-888-0321
www.craftsetc.com

Craft Site Directory
Useful online resource
www.craftsitedirectory.com

Create For Less
866-333-4463
www.createforless.com

Cia's Palette
4155 Grand Ave S.
Minneapolis
MN 55409
612-229-5227
www.ciaspalette.com

Hobby Lobby
Stores nationwide
www.hobbylobby.com

Jo-ann Fabric & Crafts
888-739-4120
www.joann.com

Micaels
Stores nationwide
www.michaels.com

Old Fashioned Milk Paint Co.
866-350-6455
www.milkpaint.com

Panduro Hobby
Online craft supplies
www.pandurohobby.com

Purl Patchwork
147 Sullivan Street
New York
NY 10012
212-420-8798
www.purlsoho.com

Reprodepot Fabrics
413-527-4047
www.reprodepotfabrics.com

S&S Worldwide Craft Supplies
800-288-9941
www.ssww.com

Sunshine Crafts
800-729-2878
www.sunshinecrafts.com

Tinsel Trading Company
47 West 38th Street
New York
NY 10018
212-730-1030
www.tinseltrading.com

Z and S Fabrics
681 S. Muddy Creek Road
Denver
PA 17157
717-336-4028
www.zandsfabrics.com

index

For Laurie Dahl. Here's to lots more lovely Christmases together.

I would like to thank the following people for their help with this book:
Debbie Patterson for the beautiful photography and for getting into the Christmas
spirit so well and Michael Hill for creating such lovely illustrations.

Roger Hammond for the great design and to Marion Paull for being an all round
lovely editor. Sally Powell at CICO for all the help and support given and to Cindy
Richards for commissioning me to do this book in the first place and encouraging
my glittery side to come out.

And finally to Laurie, Gracie, and Betty for all the encouragement, support, and love
given during our extended "Christmas." Thank you, my loves.